4O
WEEKS

Also from Heather Doyle Fraser

Daily Gratitude and Intention Journal: An Abundant Life

The *Daily Gratitude and Intention Journal* gives you an opportunity to create a formal practice of gratitude and intention setting while simultaneously rewiring your brain to see the positivity and abundance in our daily lives.

It compliments *40 Weeks: A Daily Journey of Inspiration and Abundance* by giving more structure to your morning rituals.

Available on amazon.com and CalliopeHousePress.com

4O WEEKS

A Daily Journey of
Inspiration and Abundance

HEATHER DOYLE FRASER

Calliope House Press

Copyright © 2015 by Heather Doyle Fraser
www.beyondchangecoach.com

Published 2015

Copyeditor: Bridie O'Shaughnessy
Cover Design: Danielle Baird
Book Design: Danielle Baird
Photo Credit (author photo): Todd M. Rensi

Printed in the United States of America

ISBN–13: 978–0–6925–9982–2
ISBN–10: 0–692–59982–7

First Edition

Calliope House Press — Dublin, Ohio
www.CalliopeHousePress.com

*This book is dedicated to my husband,
Chris and my daughter, Eva.*

*Without you, my life would not be nearly
so abundant or inspired.*

I love you.

TABLE OF CONTENTS

a time of
OPENING

a time of
ALLOWING

a time of
RELEASING

a time of
EMBRACING

INTRODUCTION

This book is a window into my soul.

I have always loved devotional books where you have 365 days of inspiration in which to immerse yourself. In fact, I always have at least one of these books on my bedside table. And so, naturally, I wanted to write one for myself. That's how this book began — as a meditation for myself. Each day, I would write about what I needed and what I wanted to remind myself. It became a blueprint for me of how I wanted to live my life, and how I wanted to show up day after day.

But how could I be sure that the themes I was writing about would be relevant for others? To answer this question, I started interviewing people. I talked to people all over the world about what inspired them and what brought joy and meaning to their lives. Common threads emerged: nature, music, art, relationships, connectedness, love. You will see these universal themes prominently featured throughout the book.

What else will you see?

As a transformational life coach, I am able to witness the rawness and the beauty of the human spirit every day. I see the duality of us all in every choice we make. And so, you will see a lot of that in this book.

You will also see different types of entries: active declarations for living a life that serves your highest good, poetry, quotes that speak to the heart, and observations of my own life and the lives of those around me. I purposely created a book that has variation because that's what I like. I enjoy shifting perspective. I enjoy rearranging the furniture in my life. I smile when I see or experience something a little unexpected, so that's what I aimed to create with this book.

Why 40 Weeks?

Once I was about half way through the writing, I realized something. 365 days — a year — didn't feel quite right to me. I began reflecting on the people I work with in my coaching practice, and I also started thinking about the changes I have made in my life — particularly those made in the past five years. They occur in cycles and seasons of time. Sometimes swiftly and sometimes slowly, but they all result in the generation of something new. A time frame came into my mind — 9 Months: 40 Weeks. The birth of a new life. The transformation or transmutation into something more or different.

As I began to explore this idea, I also realized that the transformations and changes that I have the privilege to witness regularly as a coach follow patterns: a time of Opening, a time of Allowing, a time of Releasing, and a time of Embracing. And so, the book naturally fell into four parts or sections — one for each season of change and transformation. These parts are each comprised of 10 weeks.

Of course, sometimes we find ourselves experiencing change and transformation in different ways. We may truly be in a time of opening, and yet, we are required to release that which doesn't serve us. You will find that each part will help you navigate these overlaps as well.

How do you want to use this book?

There are a few different ways to use this book. Obviously, you can read one entry per day for 40 weeks. Alternately, you could go to a specific section if you want an entry that relates to the season in which you currently find yourself — Opening, Allowing, Releasing, or Embracing. Still another method would be to just randomly open the book and see what comes forth for you on that particular day. All of these options (and any others that you devise) will work to give you a touchstone or an anchor at the beginning of your day.

I hope that this book brings you joy, comfort, inspiration, a feeling of abundance, and a sense of self-awareness. I hope it is something you look forward to as part of your morning ritual — perhaps before you get out of bed, or maybe as you have your morning tea, coffee, or glass of water. I hope this book gives a joyful and hopeful cadence to your days and allows you to set intentions and committed actions that serve your highest good.

If you would like to deepen your practice with this book, you can use it in conjunction with the *40 Weeks Companion Journal and Workbook.*

This is available in a downloadable and printable format on my website at
www.beyondchangecoach.com
or in a print version on www.amazon.com.

a time of

OPENING

WEEK 1

Your life begins again — now —
with the intake of your very next breath.

You probably didn't even notice
it happening, and yet, you inhaled and
began again or just continued...
it's a matter of perspective.

You can begin anew now.

Step into growth and transformation
or stay in the safety of sameness — the
choice is yours each and every moment.

a time of OPENING

WEEK 1
DAY 2

Bring your awareness today to the essence of your personal growth and transformation.

You are becoming.

Look for expansion and abundance, and you
will see the opportunity waiting for you.

As you step into your authentic self,
others will see you and begin to awake
to their own voice.

As you acknowledge
and act on the potential in your life,
you will be an inspiration.

What if that someone you inspire today
is you?

Embrace the inspiration within you.

a time of OPENING

Heather Doyle Fraser

WEEK 1
DAY 4

"SET YOUR LIFE ON FIRE. SEEK THOSE WHO FAN YOUR FLAMES."

— Rumi

40 weeks: A Daily Journey of Inspiration and Abundance

Who surrounds you?

How do you feel when you are with them?
After you leave them?

Today, notice how you cultivate your time.
Do you spend it with people who fill you
up, motivate, and inspire you or people
who deplete you and convince you to stay
small?

a time of OPENING

Heather Doyle Fraser

You have a choice.

Seek out your inspiration.

What do you really want out of life today?

Most of the time, we don't pause to even
consider what we want
on such a broad yet simple scale.

Your challenge today... reflect upon what
you really want your day to look like:

Who do you want to be?

How do you need to show up in order to
manifest your desires?

I think it's time to be a creator.

a time of OPENING

Heather Doyle Fraser

WEEK 2

In the still moments there is a knowing...
a whisper of things to come.

Listen.

a time of OPENING

Empty your pockets.

Let all of the obligations and traps
fall away.

The ones that do not serve you.
The ones that do not allow you to move
forward.
The ones that keep you up at night and
wake you in the morning with their
incessant shoulds.

Feel the lightness in your body as you
open and release that which does not
support you.

Reach inside your truth and look with fierce commitment at the person waiting.

Examine the beauty, the sorrow, the strengths, and the uniqueness that is you.

a time of OPENING

Heather Doyle Fraser

WEEK 2
DAY 4

Nature is my magic.
Constantly sending me messages,
reviving my soul,
calming my frenzied mind.
Everything becomes clear
as I walk unfettered in the sun
or in the gray shadow of twilight.
It makes no difference to my willing heart.

"THE LOVE THAT FLOWS THROUGH YOUR HEART PURIFIES NOT ONLY YOUR OWN SPIRIT, BUT THE LOVE YOU SHARE WITH OTHERS."

— Carolyn Myss

Heather Doyle Fraser

WEEK 2
DAY 6

See the love in yourself.

Look for the love in others.

Share the love you experience with everyone you meet.

Trying is a partial promise
that we make — sometimes —
when we feel like it,
when we aren't too tired or exhausted from
whatever is happening in our lives.

I want you to feel
the pleasure of commitment
and release the baggage
that comes with trying.

What is your commitment today?
It doesn't have to be big.
Start small if that feels good.

Be emboldened.

a time of OPENING

Heather Doyle Fraser

WEEK 3

What am I willing to take responsibility for
in my life right now?

Everything?

If I were to take responsibility for
everything — since I am capable of
choosing how I react to people, places, and
situations —
how would that change things for me?

I can't say in all certainty what would
change for me in the future,
but at this moment,
with this knowledge...

I am empowered.

Will you join me?

a time of OPENING

Listen with the intensity of a child.

The birdsong is there — its melody light and unbothered by the worries of the day.

Look around you.

The sun makes its way into every corner of our existence. Even in the shadow you can still see the light.

"TO MAKE A DEEP MENTAL PATH, WE MUST THINK OVER AND OVER THE KIND ⸰ THOUGHTS WE WISH TO DOMINATE OUR LIVES."

— Henry David Thoreau

a time of OPENING

Heather Doyle Fraser

The path that most of us create in our minds — what we tell ourselves minute by minute — is not necessarily what we would practice in our lives if we were given the choice. And yet, we are given the choice every day and every moment.

We allow our non-action or action that doesn't serve us to take priority. This way of being becomes a pattern and we practice it daily, hoping for a different outcome. Hoping, with all of the fear and the worry, that eventually we will feel content, safe, easeful, and at peace.

Today, I am offering another way.
Instead of practicing fear, worry, and anxiety over the past and the future, let's commit to the present.

Breathe.

Feel the peace and contentment you can create in this very moment with practice.

What if failure were an illusion?
What if we have created the concept of
failure in our minds to keep us from living
the most full and abundant lives possible?

What if everything were just an opportunity
to learn and grow?
If I can take the learning and growth with
me, maybe I can just let go of the rest.
The rest is what really holds us back: the
fear, the judgment, and the uncertainty.

What if you were willing to let all of that go
just for today
and look for the opportunity?

What would you see?

What would you do?

a time of OPENING

Heather Doyle Fraser

WEEK 3
DAY 6

Our words and actions —
our daily patterns and habits —
define who we are
moment by moment.

How are you showing up?

What if the way
to centering and grounding
was as simple as breathing?
What if you could connect any time
to that joy inside of you?

It is possible — the opportunity and
potential is at the threshold.
As you take this next breath,
feel the connection
to your purpose and your passion.

Take one step toward making your heart's
desires a reality today.

a time of OPENING

Heather Doyle Fraser

WEEK 4

I am surrounded by guides.
Their light dances around me...
leading me to the edge of leaning inward,
leading me to promises yet unspoken,
leading me beyond reason and logic
to myself.

We assign meaning to everything in our
lives every day.

We decide
what is important...
what takes priority...
what is lovely...
what is challenging...

Knowing this, I intentionally choose where
my focus and attention rest.

"OUT BEYOND IDEAS
OF WRONGDOING AND
RIGHTDOING THERE
IS A FIELD.

I'LL MEET YOU THERE.

WHEN THE SOUL LIES
DOWN IN THAT GRASS
THE WORLD IS TOO FULL
TO TALK ABOUT."

— Rumi

a time of OPENING

WEEK 4
DAY 4

Are you consciously creating your life?

It is a choice:

what you do
in this moment and the next...

how you respond or react
to situations as they arise...

the love and support you show
to yourself and others in times of
celebration and in times of distress...

What will you choose today?
To consciously create
or to apathetically be led
by the busy-ness of the day?

I am choosing creation.
Come with me into a place of flourishing.

Alignment
to our values and
to our authentic selves
brings an ease
that cannot be counterfeited.

When we feel dissonance or anxiety in
our bodies it is a sign that we are not in
alignment.

Sometimes, though, when I am following
my true path, taking the next right step,
I feel that anxiety, and it is confusing.

And then I remember:
I am pushing the boundaries. I am doing
and being what I thought at one point
wasn't possible.

I can choose to feel into
the potential and the possibility
that wasn't there before and
still feel ease.

a time of OPENING

Heather Doyle Fraser

Harmony...

that rapturous moment
when two or more tones
come together in blended perfection.

I see harmony in my life,
moment by moment, until it stretches into
and over all of my moments.

Even when the discord comes through, it
cannot take up all of the space in my life...

because... it's not what I want.

I want rapturous, joyous moments strung
together in a melody that defines my life.

I choose to make the harmony and be an
active participant.

What is your choice today?

What is one small step you can make today that will bring you more harmony and alignment?

Heather Doyle Fraser

WEEK 5

"YOU FIND PEACE
NOT BY REARRANGING
THE CIRCUMSTANCES
OF YOUR LIFE, BUT
BY REALIZING WHO
YOU ARE AT THE
DEEPEST LEVEL."

— Eckhart Tolle

a time of OPENING

WEEK 5
DAY 2

Who are you at the deepest level?

Can you see it in yourself?

What are you an ambassador of at this place in your life?

Settle in and ask yourself,
"What do I want to bring to my life
and the lives of others every day?"

Transformation often comes hand in hand
with discomfort, at least at the beginning.

At the start, change can feel uncomfortable
— it's not what we know. Change that
becomes transformation requires us to dig
deep and shine a light on parts of us that
are painful or vulnerable.

AND

In shining that light on our vulnerabilities
and our rawness we are able to see with
clear eyes where we need to go and what
might be the best next step.

What discomfort are you willing to
experience today to move you forward into
growth and the life you want?

a time of OPENING

WEEK 5
DAY 4

You have a choice in how you perceive
yourself and your place in the world today.

What words will you use to describe
yourself, your situation, your
circumstances?

I am an ambassador of Joy,
Transformation, Light, and Ease.

I choose Joy.

I choose Transformation.

I choose to be the Light in a dark place.

I choose Ease.

What will you choose?

The duality of snow.
Beautiful, pristine as it comes down
each flake unique in its making.
Unyielding
as it blankets the space around me.
I yearn to disturb the perfect white
that covers my surroundings.
I yearn to venture out
and see the beauty it holds.
I am willing to experience the cold and
difficult passage to see the magic.

Later,
when I look out on my own footprints
I realize —
I am not a straight-line-kind-of-person.
I meander.
I look for what lies beneath —
the subtle shifts and changes
that can only be seen
with keen, dedicated observation,
quiet reflection, and a slow pace.
And there it is... the magic.

a time of OPENING

Heather Doyle Fraser

"SIMPLICITY IS NOT
A GOAL, BUT ONE
ARRIVES AT SIMPLICITY
IN SPITE OF ONESELF,
AS ONE APPROACHES
THE REAL MEANING
OF THINGS."

— Herbert Read

As you get closer to the truth for yourself,
situations and circumstances become simple.
The complexities we once thought we knew
are replaced with an inner knowing that
eradicates drama and confusion.

That doesn't mean that simplicity is always
easy. But, what if it could be?

What if we could make every situation
simpler by asking ourselves this one
glorious question,

"What can I do to make this easier?"

Try it.

a time of OPENING

WEEK 6

The foundation of every choice is built
upon either

LOVE or FEAR.

Are you building an experience based
on love?

Challenge yourself today to come into
each choice, experience, and interaction
with love.

"WE ATTRACT EXPERIENCES THAT ARE CONSISTENT WITH OUR BELIEFS."

— Arielle Ford

We see what we want to see and what we
expect to see every moment of every day.

Why not set an expectation to see the best
the world has to offer?

If you look hard enough,
you will find it...
again... and... again...

WEEK 6
DAY 4

That little voice that talks to you when you're tired and overwhelmed? We all have one — it's our inner critic — and we don't need to believe everything it tells us.

The inner critic wants to stay in safety and sameness, but you can create a different story.

Start where you are. What's in your story today?

Rituals and routines are important for creating new helpful patterns in your life and shedding those that no longer serve you.

Do something for yourself today that serves you fully. It can be as simple as showing yourself compassion and kindness when you most need it.

Be intentional.

What will you do today?

a time of OPENING

WEEK 6
DAY 6

Dance today.

Feel the music within you and around you.

Dance with softness and passion.

Dance with abandon and timidity.

Dance with your eyes closed and
wide open.

"ALL GREAT CHANGES ARE PRECEDED BY CHAOS."

— Deepak Chopra

WEEK 7

I feel the chaos in my life

and

I allow the change to enfold me.

I am a willing participant in my own
transformation.

What a beautiful perspective.

Joy and transformation
are always inside of us,
but sometimes we forget.

Remember today...

Remember joy...

Remember to sing...

Remember to dance...

Remember to love...

Remember to create...

Remember your abundance...

"WE ARE SHAPED & FASHIONED BY WHAT WE LOVE."

— Johann Wolfgang Von Goethe

What do you love?

Who do you love?

Are the people, situations, and
circumstances that surround you building
you up and making you a better person

OR

are they tearing you down
and keeping you from your best self?

The fog is thick this morning,
obscuring what I know to be true.
And when I can't see
the firm shapes before me
I look for anything else
to make sense of the landscape.

As the sun rises,
soft shifts in color emerge —
the cloudy white revealing soft orange,
pink, and yellow fuzzy shimmer in the fog.
I can make something of this day.

a time of OPENING

Heather Doyle Fraser

Do you feel fear or tension when faced with change or the unknown?

We all do at one time or another.

You are not alone.

How can you dance
with that uncertainty today,
and live in concert with it?

Take back your power.

You may have given it away to a person, a
situation or an emotion without realizing it.

Retrieve it with your heart.

Embody it with your soul.

a time of OPENING

WEEK 8

"ENVISION POSSIBILITY.

Don't worry who else believes in it; the universe is only looking for instructions from you."

— Marianne Williamson

WEEK 8
DAY 2

Possibility, potential, and opportunity are waiting for you every day, every moment. Being open to seeing these gems is your job.

Can you flip your perspective today?

Where is your possibility?

Look for it.

Create your abundant life...

choice by choice,

step by step.

What gives you purpose and meaning?

What speaks to you now?

Collaborate with your highest self
to create something
purposeful and meaningful.

Reach into your heart and find the passion
you need to begin.

a time of OPENING

WEEK 8
DAY 4

Just breathe.

And allow the unfolding.

Make your choices today and know that you are doing the best you can do with the tools you have.

You are enough.

Let negative emotions come...
and then...
pass by,

all the while
grounding yourself
in love, compassion, and your breath.

You can choose to let love be the
foundation for your day.

a time of OPENING

Heather Doyle Fraser

"BEHIND THE CLICHE
THAT YOU CREATE
YOUR OWN REALITY
IS A SHADOW;
IF YOU DON'T CREATE
YOUR OWN REALITY,
IT WILL BE CREATED
FOR YOU."

— Deepak Chopra

What are you creating today?

Envision your highest goals and ideals and move toward that amazing reality one step at a time.

Start now.

WEEK 9

There's a maple tree
that watches over me
right outside my door.
Her face is knowing —
has she been there these ten years?
Or did she just suddenly appear
when I saw her yesterday?

Her eyes are fierce yet compassionate;
they see into me and around me.
Her smile serene;
I can feel her caress as I walk past or
linger beneath her branches.
It doesn't matter when she came.
She is here to be a witness
for me and my family.
Her nurturance
bending over us in this house.
I feel her presence as I come and go
and I am comforted.

a time of OPENING

Change...

We can embrace it and
be open to the opportunities that arise

OR

we can resist and stay in the safety of
sameness.

What is your choice today?

"FEAR IS EXCITEMENT WITHOUT THE BREATH."

— Gay Hendricks

Heather Doyle Fraser

It is so much more empowering
to think of myself as
excited with anticipation
about what might be coming
rather than as fearful
about what might be coming.

It's just a lens I use to help me see my life
more clearly.

AND

I do more because of it.

Awake.

Your greatness is there within you waiting
for your acknowledgement and action.

Your opportunity is now...

Start planting and nourishing
the seeds of your new creation.

a time of OPENING

Be Brave.

Be Bold.

Be Kind.

Be Compassionate.

Be Thoughtful.

Be Intentional.

Be You.

Once I thought my life would follow

a path that I could name...

a path that would be predictable...

As it turns out,
I'm creating the path every day as I walk,
run, jump or crawl my next step.

And I don't know what the end will be yet...

Isn't that WONDERFUL?

a time of OPENING

WEEK 10

Open.

Open to your self.

Open to your body.

Open to your heart.

Open to your soul.

Open.

As you move
through your day,
pay particular attention
to the blessings around you
with their wonder and imperfections
together.

Slow down today.

See and hear with an open heart.

Savor each moment as it comes.

Taste the day.

Touch its radiance.

Feel into its abundance.

Embrace your becoming.

a time of OPENING

"POTENTIAL IS THE UNIVERSE STANDING ON THE EDGE OF THE LEAPING PLACE CALLING TO YOU AND SAYING, I'M READY FOR YOU."

— David Robinson

So, the question, then, is...

Are you READY?

Fly into your potential and possibility.

What does this wind have to say to me?
Blustery and unyielding,
it moves me down the street —
not unkindly —
but too forcefully for my taste.

This frenetic pace leaves me wondering
what will happen
if I stay in the wind longer.
Will I swirl around like the leaves —
not going much of anywhere,
not seeing which way is here or there,
but moving nonetheless?
It's exciting and exhilarating
as it almost takes my breath away,
but I think I will seek refuge
in a slower pace,
in the sheltered space between houses,
where I can catch my breath
and see what lies ahead.

a time of OPENING

Heather Doyle Fraser

Make a deep connection with
someone today.

Be curious about what brings them
joy and fulfillment
and celebrate their greatness.

Physical and emotional discomfort is
temporary.

If you feel pain or tension today, breathe
through these sensations and know that
change is constant.

Transformation is right around the corner
with purposeful intention and focused
action.

And...

In this place where you feel discomfort —
in this place where healing is beginning —
be gentle and kind with yourself.
Show yourself the loving kindness you
would show to a child, a dear friend, a
partner, or a beloved animal.

a time of OPENING

Heather Doyle Fraser

a time of

ALLOWING

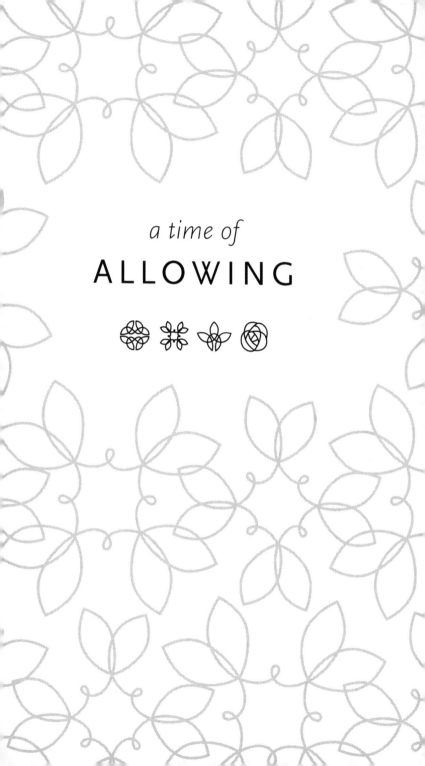

WEEK 11

How do you intend to spend your
time today?

Is it in the service of the people and the
values that make you whole?

Who are the people that surround you on a
regular basis?
Do they fill you and lift you up?
Do they hold space for you to see
possibility and potential?
Do they inspire you to be the best version
of yourself?

a time of ALLOWING

WEEK 11
DAY 2

Take time to connect with someone who
inspires you.

Notice how intentional connection with
someone magical feels in your body
and heart.

What are your morning rituals?

Everyone has them —
things they do every day that
create a calm in the chaos —
but some people create morning rituals
with meaning. And these rituals become a
grounding force in the start of their days.

Think about how you start your mornings.
If what you do isn't serving you, reflect on
what would bring some ease and joy at the
start of your day.

a time of ALLOWING

WEEK 11
DAY 4

Cultivating a daily practice of gratitude is
a good way to inspire yourself to powerful
intention setting and committed actions.

The more you practice gratitude formally,
the more it changes your being.
You begin to see all things as a gift or a
path to learning. It re-wires your brain to
look for how events in our lives can help us
rather than hurt us.

Today, write down three things for which
you are grateful and why.
And then tomorrow, do it again.

Freedom rests within you.

Heather Doyle Fraser

WEEK 11
DAY 6

Notice what is happening in your body
today. You may be feeling tension or
discomfort, or you may revel in the overall
strength and flexibility of your body.

Wherever you fall on the continuum,
breathe into all of your splendor. If you
notice any tension, discomfort or pain,
focus your breath and attention to this area
of your body. Feel the release — whether it
is a small ripple or a massive wave.

Allow whatever comes up and savor
the physical feelings and emotions that
surface. Surrender to the release and to the
natural state of joy within you, even if it is a
pinprick of light at this moment.

Allow...
Surrender...
Release...

Whatever feelings and emotions come
up today are just what you need at this
moment.

Use these three words as a mantra:
Allow...
Surrender...
Release...

With each breath you are creating an
understanding and learning within you.

Again and again.

a time of ALLOWING

WEEK 12

Oh, that I could wander with you
in the pale soft light of the morning
whispering our secret longings
and big dreams
knowing we are safe.

a time of ALLOWING

There is so much in this life that
we feel we need to control.
It brings us a sense of calm.
Control feels safe and known.
This is why we grasp at control —
of others, of situations, of the future.

And for the most part, control is an illusion.

We can only control our choices, our
actions, our behaviors, and our responses.

Time spent trying to control more is futile.
It leads not to safety and certainty, but to
tightness and constriction.

What would your day look like if you made
a commitment to release your control of
others and the situations in which you find
yourself?

What if your focus shifted inwards towards
your responses and reactions?

Do you ever hear yourself saying, "I will be happy when..."

We spend a lot of time focusing on what we don't have and looking forward to a future that holds peace, contentment, well-being, happiness, and abundance.

But what if this abundance is already around us and we just aren't seeing it?

What if the contentment and well-being are small and sitting alongside the chaos of our daily experience?

a time of ALLOWING

WEEK 12
DAY 4

What if we looked for joy and abundance
— however small — and focused on the
beauty of that smallness?

What if our attention allowed that peace,
contentment, and joy to grow even amidst
chaos and uncertainty?

Take off your blinders. Allow your joy to
root itself in every breath.

Be a gentle whisper...
an easy waterfall into a flowing stream.

Water is powerful even in its gentleness.
It yields, and yet is unyielding.
Its persistence is unwavering.

a time of ALLOWING

Heather Doyle Fraser

"DO NOT GO WHERE THE PATH MAY LEAD; GO INSTEAD WHERE THERE IS NO PATH AND LEAVE A TRAIL."

— Ralph Waldo Emerson

What if you could access joy and
abundance every day?

See it, taste it, feel it, hear it, and smell it
with all of your being in each moment.

Let it infiltrate your life.

It is here. It is within your reach NOW.

You are ready. This is your time.

a time of ALLOWING

WEEK 13

What if allowing your joy and greatness to emerge replaced your need for perfection?

What if acknowledging the greatness and the gifts within you was the first step to releasing the illusion of perfection?

What would you be free to create... to be... to do... after that first step?

a time of ALLOWING

You have a direct line to your joy.
It's right there within you...
in your greatness.
in your strengths.

What if that acknowledgement alone
gave you permission to stop focusing on
the outcomes and instead focus on the
creation, the process, and the practice of
your life?

What small things could you do differently
with this shift in perspective?

Every shift, every change makes a
difference.

A shift in perspective is just what we all need
most of the time.

With that shift, suddenly, the situation that
has kept us up all night becomes something
different.
Our relationship to it changes.
We change as we relate to it.

With that beautiful shift, a problem
transforms into a challenge or an adventure.

Pain and sadness become learning for the
future and therefore useful.

Time becomes a gift and a luxury rather than
our enemy.

If you want a shift in perspective, choose to
see one. Look for it underneath or alongside
all of the noise and chatter.

It's there... waiting.

a time of ALLOWING

Heather Doyle Fraser

I was walking today among the trees.
Some were robust and yielding
bountiful growth, others were broken,
their limbs tired or gone completely.
Some were nearly brand new —
delicate but strong with their branches
reaching towards the sun.
Others were old, standing or halfway fallen,
but only a husk of their former selves.
I spent some time resting at one such tree.
And I noticed...
the moss grew thick at the base.
The tree I had dismissed
was still serving a purpose.
The moss was teeming with life,
bursting with color, creating a forest
of breath and beauty
right here in this place
I had thought barren.

"EVERY DAY IS A GOOD DAY WHEN YOU PAINT."

— Bob Ross

a time of ALLOWING

The frenzy is all around us...
and yet, so is the peace, calm,
contentment, and joy.

What do you feel on a daily basis?

Do you feel the pull of the chaos and then
suddenly find yourself speeding up to
match and join its pace? Sometimes we
allow ourselves to be carried away by the
energy and the force of others, even if this
isn't what we want.

This is precisely the time to
slow down,
breathe,
listen...
and then make an intentional choice.

Breathe.

Just like that.

Again and again.

WEEK 14

Create an adventure... just for today.

Allow the tapestry to coax you, enfold you.
Let the colors delight you and challenge you.
Embrace your doubts and hold hands with
your fear.

Play in the vibrancy of your life.

a time of ALLOWING

Allow your curiosity to accompany you. Look on each moment with the astonishment of a beginner. Each moment is new, bright, and shining.

What if you brought that attitude of wonder and newness to each interaction, each observation, each breath?

Things might be different.

"WHEN WE FOCUS
OUR ATTENTION
IN THE HERE AND NOW
AND LIVE SIMPLY,
WE HAVE MORE TIME
TO DO THE THINGS
WE THINK ARE
IMPORTANT."

— Thic Nhat Hanh

a time of ALLOWING

Heather Doyle Fraser

Today, step out of your comfort zone.

Say YES to something new.

Just BREATHE and allow your greatness to emerge.

It's waiting there for you —
your greatness —
sometimes on the surface
of your skin
and sometimes
underneath your resistance.

Commit to fully be you.

Just for today.

Just to see how it feels to inhabit a place
where everything — all of your best parts
and all of the parts you don't like so much
— are all perfectly imperfect.

The shiny and the not-so-shiny
exist together
and make you who you are... BRILLIANT.

a time of ALLOWING

Heather Doyle Fraser

Often we allow ourselves
to become so busy that we forget...

We forget to look for and to see the joy in
our activities and interactions — in our
every day.

What if you dropped your badge of
busy-ness?

What if you allowed yourself to be
intentional today about bringing the FUN?

I see the light spreading in the morning.
First a soft glow at the edge of the horizon.
More blue and gray and lavender
in the early moments than brilliant
pinpricks or rays announcing the day.
The light comes on quietly, beckoning me
to acknowledge its beauty.
I pause and congratulate the sun and earth
on a job well done.
And then I remember that this simplicity
and exquisiteness happens every day.
I can be a witness
And allow the light to lift my spirit
and my mind to a higher place.
I can make a promise
to spread the light in soft and quiet
moments and even in a loud declaration
when it's needed.

a time of ALLOWING

Heather Doyle Fraser

WEEK 15

Where is your joy today?

It is within and around all of us... waiting to be noticed.

Be present and mindful as you go about your routine.

When you take that first sip of water, coffee, or tea in the morning, how does it feel?

When you see the first glimpse of sun peeking through your window...

When you eat...

When you walk and feel the breeze on your face...

Lovely.

a time of ALLOWING

Check in with yourself.

Notice what brings you a sense of calm.

Notice when you are excited.

Notice when you are agitated or frustrated.

And then, ask yourself,

"What am I doing when I feel most contented?"

Let's do more of that.

"The art of living does not consist in preserving and clinging to a particular mode of happiness, but in allowing happiness to change its form without being disappointed by the change;

HAPPINESS, LIKE A CHILD, MUST BE ALLOWED TO GROW UP."

— Charles Morgan

a time of ALLOWING

Heather Doyle Fraser

Look inside today as you experience difficult situations or people.

You can choose to react in anger and frustration or respond with compassion and empathy.

What if you started today with gratitude?
Think of three things—people, activities,
experiences, knowings for which you are
grateful in this moment.

Write them down.
Drink in their wonderfulness and allow
them to permeate this moment...
Feel your appreciation all the way into your
heart and soul.

a time of ALLOWING

Heather Doyle Fraser

Starting the day with gratitude and intention allows us a calm knowing of our purpose.

And, when you feel grounded in your purpose, you can make a choice about what will bring the highest good for you and those around you in this moment.

What will you commit to today?

Be gentle...

Choose love...

Show compassion...

Inhabit kindness...

Smile...

Breathe...

Create space...

    for yourself and others.

a time of ALLOWING

Heather Doyle Fraser

WEEK 16

In the quiet stillness there is a knowing.

A place of ease and contentment
waiting...
unfolding...
growing...
becoming...

a time of ALLOWING

You have greatness within you.

Allow your creative power to come through today.

I can look inside.
I can create space for all that is in me.
I can gently hold my missteps.
I can embody loving kindness for myself.
I can call myself beloved.

a time of ALLOWING

"TRUE REFUGE IS THAT WHICH ALLOWS US TO BE AT HOME, AT PEACE, TO DISCOVER TRUE HAPPINESS.

The only thing that can give us true refuge is the awareness and love that is intrinsic to who we are. Ultimately, it's our own true nature."

— Tara Brach

Today can be whatever you want it to be.

Breathe deeply.
Be grateful.
Set your intentions
for a vibrant experience — or whatever
most serves your vision for the day —
And follow with the committed actions that
will bring these intentions to life.

This is your abundant life.

a time of ALLOWING

WEEK 16
DAY 6

Shine your light today.

Allow the dimness of doubt
to slip away into the shadows.
If you find yourself falling into a pattern
that doesn't serve you
or where you want to be,
gently come back
to your heart-centered self.

Look for the light and you will find it
within you.

A challenge in a busy world: slow down to
speed up.

Take a short walk today —
just five minutes —
and notice the beauty and wonder
around you.

It's there...
in the snow or sunshine,
in the blue, gray, or multicolored sky.
in the trees, the grass, the dirt
in the architecture of the buildings or houses
on your street.
in the way that the cracks form in the
sidewalk
in the faces of the people around you —
young, old, or somewhere in between.

Be unyielding in your search.

a time of ALLOWING

Heather Doyle Fraser

WEEK 17

Things can become complicated quickly...
but what if today were easy?

Sometimes when things seem hard and
every action I take feels like a struggle to
me, I ask myself how I can make things
easier. And then, I wait and listen.

I know in my heart where I need to slow
down or shift my energy. I know what will
lift me up and what will bring vitality.

What would that look like and feel like?
Stop and imagine yourself moving through
your day with ease and energy.
See yourself flowing from one conversation
to the next and one situation or
circumstance to the next.

Ahhh... ease.

a time of ALLOWING

Savor each moment today...
the aromas,
your dear one's voice,
a smile given freely,
the feel of the air on your face,
the taste of your food,
that peculiar blue of the sky that fills you
with awe.

What if you treated each moment with
reverence? What if you made the cuddle on
the couch or the act of walking outside to
get your mail important?

What would change for you today?

In the stillness
there is calm and peace.

Go there today
with your breath
and with your heart.
It will be your solace.

a time of ALLOWING

Heather Doyle Fraser

"STOP ACTING SO SMALL. YOU ARE THE UNIVERSE IN ECSTATIC MOTION."

— Rumi

Everyone wants to experience fulfillment,
joy, and a purpose- or passion-driven life.

But sometimes this seems so far away.

Fulfillment comes from living intentionally
and authentically as often as possible.

Be you. All of you.

a time of ALLOWING

Heather Doyle Fraser

Curious, these colors in the sky.
A thin line of vibrant tangerine separates
the most calming ombre blue —
graduating from pale aqua to sapphire —
from a swirl of steel gray clouds.
The clouds are dark and menacing on their
own, but seen together with the vibrancy
and serenity of the orange and blue they
are transmuted into something beautiful
and grounding.

Suddenly,
the meaning of color changes
as my vision sees a fuller, richer landscape.
The view is better for the juxtaposition
of the heaviness against the lightness.
Oh that I could see this dichotomy
and rejoice in it always.

We all crave balance. And sometimes our crazy lives take over and we are left swaying.

If you feel out of balance today, take a look at where you are spending your time and with whom. Are these activities and people in alignment with what you value?

What choices can you make to support your highest self today?

a time of ALLOWING

WEEK 18

Breathe into any uncertainty, doubt, or
fear today.

Let these emotions come up.
Look at them in the face.
Smile with the knowledge that the present
moment can bring you back to yourself and
release you in its simplicity.

WEEK 18
DAY 2

Worrying and ruminating are always in relation to the past or the future.

Take back your power.
It's right here with your next breath.

We all have moments of agitation, frustration or stress. These feelings and emotions will come up, despite our fervent wishes that they would not. But, we don't have to give them the power to take over our existence.

If you feel a hostile take-over start to emerge...

Stop. Breathe.

In that quiet moment, ask what you can do right NOW to bring yourself more joy, calm, or just a little relief.

And then, do something a little different — TAKE ACTION.

a time of ALLOWING

"UNBOUNDEDNESS
AND ABUNDANCE ARE
OUR NATURAL STATE.
WE JUST NEED TO
RESTORE THE MEMORY
OF WHAT WE
ALREADY KNOW."

— Deepak Chopra

We don't always look at how far
we've come.

The beauty that we have created around us.

The greatness hiding or waiting inside
of us.

What are you celebrating today?

Acknowledge what you have accomplished
or those beautiful, unique strengths
within you.

Let this beauty motivate you to take that
next step forward.

a time of ALLOWING

Today as you grow
into that higher version of yourself,
feel the excitement and fear
at the possibility that awaits.

Experience both and JUMP!

Let your breath center you today.

Notice the beauty and abundance around
you and share it with others. If they refuse
to see it, be thankful that you can.

Send love and compassion to those around
you so that they may be able to see the
world through your eyes.

a time of ALLOWING

Heather Doyle Fraser

WEEK 19

What patterns are you reinforcing?

Sometimes we don't realize
that by passively standing by
we are reinforcing patterns
that aren't serving us.
Or sometimes we are actively reinforcing
them with the choices we make.
Either way, if you don't like how things
unfold, shift your actions, non-actions, and
your perspective.

One small change can bring a huge shift.
It can stop a pattern in its tracks and begin
to build a new one — if you are intentional
and purposeful.

Where is your change today?

a time of ALLOWING

Sometimes we need a dance break.

Move your body — even for one song — and see what happens.

Let yourself feel the music under your skin.

Let yourself dance with all your parts.

Allow an unraveling and let your heart lead.

How can you support yourself today?

Ask yourself,
"What do I need to do right now?"

And then... forge your next small step.

Gently bring yourself back to your purpose.

a time of ALLOWING

Heather Doyle Fraser

"OUR INTENTION CREATES OUR REALITY."

— Wayne Dyer

Be intentional today.

Mindfully prepare your food — savor the aroma and taste.

Close your eyes and listen to the beauty around you.

Bring in the quiet and make your choice for the day unfolding before you.

a time of ALLOWING

Listen to your intuitive wisdom.

Where can you bend to make things easier for yourself and others?

You are not alone in your struggles or your joys. With your flexibility, allow yourself to give and receive without care or reservation.

You are soft.

You are supple.

You are strong.

You are unfolding.

DAY 7

See life today with eyes of a child.

Remember your greatness — uncover it with abandon.

Listen to its song and dance to its rhythm.

Move towards possibility, beauty, and opportunity.

a time of ALLOWING

WEEK 20

Your abundant life is here,
right now, in this moment,
and in every moment of this day.

Lean in with loving and tender kindness...
embrace it.

Be intentional. Slow down.

The magic happens in the stillness.

Smell and taste your food... savor
each bite.

Listen with an undeterred focus.

Fixate your attention on something
mundane and ordinary. What do you hear
and see that you never noticed before?

Observe how it feels to be purposeful.

Give yourself a gift today of 15 minutes of quiet without distractions — no phone, no media, no doing.

Just be.

Sometimes the right action is to be still.

a time of ALLOWING

Where is your peace and calm today?

We search and search for this elusive place, only to find that it is not outside of us.

Contentment is not a rolling green meadow where we finally arrive, polished and clean, and ready to greet the day.

It is the place we come from. A place that on the surface might appear messy and complicated, but when you look deeper is just as it should be.

Simple and whole.

Unfettered and free.

Go against the grain.

Focus today on just one thing at a time.

Allow your intuitive wisdom to take over your multi-tasking hands and mind.

Notice how it feels in your body and heart to live in the present moment.

a time of **ALLOWING**

Heather Doyle Fraser

Use your body wisdom as a compass to navigate your day.

Where do you need to take action or slow down?

Listen with care and abandon both, and then, follow through.

"BEING HEARD IS SO CLOSE TO BEING LOVED THAT FOR THE AVERAGE PERSON, THEY ARE ALMOST INDISTINGUISHABLE."

— David Augsburger

a time of ALLOWING

Heather Doyle Fraser

a time of

RELEASING

WEEK 21

Make room for your pain.

We tend to want to push our pain away, but what would happen if we didn't? What would happen if we embraced our pain and held it in our hearts as we would a small child?

And then, what if you continued walking in your valued life direction, gently bringing the pain with you? When the pain has served its purpose, you can release it.

What will you embrace today so you may release it tomorrow?

a time of RELEASING

Your future is here.

Now is your time.

Act. Love. Live.

You are ready for the next step.

Nature is a great teacher.

The change of seasons, the cycles of growth, hibernation, death, and rebirth remind us that change is all around us in every moment.

What happens when you lean in to the change rather than resist it?

What if you accepted change as a natural part of your existence and allowed yourself to bend and shift as needed?

a time of RELEASING

Begin fresh.

Start something you have been resisting or delaying.

No more excuses: what is the first committed action you need to take today?

You only need to take one small step to start or continue.

Be kind to yourself...

Recharge, read, write in a journal.
Color, paint, sing, or dance.
Just BE in the way that feels the best to you
in the moment.

Practice the art of not doing.

And then, in the open space that you have
created, listen.

The sound of stillness can be beautiful.

a time of RELEASING

Heather Doyle Fraser

What stories have you created around your abundance, power, and prosperity?

We tend to carry beliefs we picked up along the way — from our parents, teachers, the world around us — and think that these beliefs are our own. We write our stories on the foundation of these beliefs when in reality, they may not be ours at all.

What are you carrying around with you every day?

Maybe it's time to take a look and make a new choice.

Maybe it's time to define your life by your rules.

Maybe it's time to create the stories that build on the foundation you have chosen, with your eyes, heart, and mind wide open.

Transformation requires movement out of
your comfort zone and
into possibility and potential.

Where is your potential today?

Ready.
Set.
STRETCH.

a time of RELEASING

Heather Doyle Fraser

WEEK 22

I am timeless.
I feel the wisdom
inside of me
brimming to the edge of wanting,
waiting for a time of giving.
This is always who I have been.
This is all I remember
as I release myself
from the shackles of the ordinary.

a time of RELEASING

Detox your day:

Go into the stillness of your heart.

Breathe in the love waiting for you.

Exhale any fear, doubt, tension, or resentment you may feel.

Then — and this is very important —

SMILE.

Be like a tree.

Breathe into your trunk.

Branch out with all your senses.

Root yourself in the present moment.

Once you are grounded, allow the richness of the soil and the nourishment of the water and sun to bring growth and healing — whatever you may need.

a time of RELEASING

Heather Doyle Fraser

WEEK 22
DAY 4

Choose your course.

There are so many options available. We may not like all that are available, but there are still choices.

That brings me immense hope.

Your job is not to figure out the how and the why.

Today, focus on just one thing — the committed, right actions you need to take in order to move forward.

What is your next step?

"WHEN OUR WILL IS STRONG AND ALIGNED WITH DIVINE INTENT, THERE IS NOTHING WE CANNOT DO OR BE.

With power and guidance flowing through us, Life becomes an effortless dance as we relinquish control and limitation and allow our Spirit Within to express itself."

—Peter Santos

Sometimes we all have days where things seem harder than we think they should be.

Remember, whenever you begin to feel the strain of struggle, you have a choice.

Stop. Breathe.

Ask the question, "What can I do to make things easier for myself today?"

Start there, with that very first thought and allow what comes forth as you tune in to your inner wisdom.

Today could be easy.

a time of RELEASING

WEEK 23

Sometimes the body becomes tired or physically depleted before we experience more difficult challenges.

It can feel the rising tension and stress and responds accordingly, wanting to prepare itself for what lies ahead.

Your body is a compass — listen to and honor its wisdom.

Nurture yourself as much as possible with healing foods, water, rest, and a whole lot of love.

a time of RELEASING

Imagine a day
where everything falls away
but that which is truly important.

Imagine a day
where the temperature is just right
the breeze caresses your skin,
and the sun warms your face.

Imagine a day
where you are heard and seen,
valued and loved.

Imagine a day
where you feel joy, excitement,
fulfillment and accomplishment,
and every emotion

that will serve you.

What can you do today to bring yourself
more ease?

What can you do to create the day that lives
in your imagination?

Bring yourself back to your breath.
Be in this moment.
Release your expectation.
Love.
Live.

a time of RELEASING

Heather Doyle Fraser

WEEK 23
DAY 4

Even in the night
there is a light
that calls to me
as I fall into dreams.
A light that beckons
hope and longing both...

Sometimes I am afraid
of what I might see in the dark.
And then I remember
there is always the light.

Gently ask someone
you care deeply about,
"What can I do to make your life easier today?"

And then... surprise that dear soul.
Lovingly and joyfully serve this person
you love.

Bring to them a piece of heaven.
Let their longing be quenched.

a time of RELEASING

Heather Doyle Fraser

If joy and abundance were a part of your every day, how would that change you?

What would you do differently right now?

Love is always the way...

In mindfully returning back to our love
again and again,
we can joyfully embrace both the shadow
and the light of this world.

a time of RELEASING

Heather Doyle Fraser

WEEK 24

Transformation requires not only growth
and action, but also nurturance.

Today, make space to be still and
honor all of the changes you are making.

a time of RELEASING

What is your next right action?

Listen to your heart in
the stillness you create...
with your breath
with your attention
with your intention
amidst the clamorous call of busy.

Where is your possibility and
potential today?

Step out of your fear and into that
opportunity with the knowledge that you
can create what you desire.

Heather Doyle Fraser

"AT THE HEIGHT OF LAUGHTER, THE UNIVERSE IS FLUNG INTO A KALEIDOSCOPE OF NEW POSSIBILITIES."

— Jean Houston

Look for your dreams
with focused abandon
and you will find them
waiting for you
to light the flame.

Heather Doyle Fraser

Your perception
defines your reality.

Your focus and intention
define your reality.

Your actions, committed and purposeful,
or haphazard and unintentional
define your reality.

What will you make of today?

What will you choose?

If you don't like how things have begun,
reset and start fresh.

You can always begin again.

I see you
   sitting there

believing in something
   outside of you.

Shift to the song within.

That melody is richer and has
more meaning than anything
you could find outside of yourself.

Heather Doyle Fraser

WEEK 25

What is important to you?

What values most define you at this
moment in your life?

I am an ambassador of...
Joy. Transformation. Ease.

What if you declared yourself right here,
right now?

What if you committed to being the
ambassador that lives within you?

There are no rules for your ambassadorship.
Sometimes you may show up silently with
small actions and gestures that inspire
others, and sometimes you may show
up with a fervor that cannot be quieted,
your voice igniting the passions of those
around you.

How will you show up today?

a time of RELEASING

Come back
to the stillness of your heart.
Rest in the present moment
and breathe in
the abundance around you.

Your true, lovely, courageous self
is waiting for you
to come home.

Freedom.

Safety.

We think about it all the time without even realizing it. We are hard-wired to look for the danger and pay attention to our fears. This attention and focus keeps us safe.

And over time the safety zone becomes our comfort zone.

Sometimes our comfort zone is just where we need to be. And other times we need to stretch out of the safety of sameness and into possibility.

What will you stretch into today?

a time of RELEASING

"GLORIOUSNESS AND WRETCHEDNESS NEED EACH OTHER. ONE INSPIRES US, THE OTHER SOFTENS US. THEY GO TOGETHER."

— Pema Chödrön

We all need help now and then. We all crave a sense of unity and togetherness. And, if we're being honest, no one does everything on their own every day.

You may receive an unexpected helping hand on the way out to your car.
Someone may offer to hold a door for you when your hands are full.
A friend might offer to take your resume to her employer because she thinks you would be a perfect fit at her company and you are suffering in your job.
A spouse or partner may offer to do the dishes, laundry, or some task that is difficult for you on a day when you are overloaded.

Today, reach out to someone in need and ask yourself what you could do to bring some ease. And then, in that support of someone else, be open to receive for yourself.

a time of RELEASING

Heather Doyle Fraser

Receiving.

Sometimes that can be hard to allow.
We are so attached to hard work and
difficulties and challenge. And when we
experience something that is easy we often
dismiss it. If it's not hard or challenging
or difficult, it must not be as valid or as
worthy.

It could be easy because you are specifically
suited to the task. Your gifts, talents,
strengths, and experience made you
capable of handling the situation. It could
be easy because someone helped you and
that made all of the difference.

What if you looked for opportunity,
possibility, and potential today instead of
looking for ways that your day might be
challenging or difficult? What if you opened
your mind to the possibility of receiving?

What would your life be like if you didn't
engage with self-judgment or criticism?

Today, you could simply acknowledge its
presence and nothing more.

You could hear
that negative and punishing refrain
and then slow down.

You could breathe.

You could choose
to replace the unhelpful thought
with one that is kind and generous.

You could choose
to show yourself loving kindness.

You could choose
to let go.

a time of RELEASING

Heather Doyle Fraser

WEEK 26

"LOVE RECOGNIZES NO BARRIERS. IT JUMPS HURDLES, LEAPS FENCES, PENETRATES WALLS TO ARRIVE AT ITS DESTINATION FULL OF HOPE."

—Maya Angelou

a time of RELEASING

WEEK 26
DAY 2

Strength lives
in your vulnerability.
        Embrace it today.

Experience your emotions
and grow in your strength.

Let their release help and heal you.

The stars whisper to me,
"We are connected, you and I."

And I whisper back, "I know."

Heather Doyle Fraser

If everything is an opportunity
to help you grow and transform into your
most wondrous, beautiful self,
there is nothing that can stop you.

Embrace your mistakes and missteps.
They come to you for a reason.

Learn from them and start fresh, like a
morning breaking out of the dark.

Have you ever watched a sunrise?

It is always magnificently beautiful, each one
different. Sometimes coming in fiery with
orange and pink and purple, and other days
coming in on a whisper in blues and grays and
white with a touch of yellow around the edges.
And still other days it comes in one way —
maybe in a calm, unassuming gray — and
then explodes into color just minutes later.

And it starts in the darkness.
Every sunrise starts in the darkness.

And then this beauty ushers in a new day
without apology, without explanation.

Become beauty today...
    without apology...
    without explanation...

and then
    watch the sun rise.

a time of RELEASING

Heather Doyle Fraser

Freedom

It's something we all yearn for —
freedom to be who we are,
freedom to do what we want.
And I find that for me, freedom equals ease.

So maybe
it is not a place to search out.
Maybe
it is not a place to finally arrive.
Maybe instead,
it is a place to come from.

That thought comforts and calms me. It
takes away my yearning. Freedom is inside
of me, alongside me, all around me.

I am willing to make choices that support
my own freedom.

I am willing to make my life easier today.

Come back to yourself.

Savor.

Show gratitude.

Breathe deeply.

Move your body.

Notice the divine in the every day —
in loving words,
random acts of kindness,
smiles,
the sun shining suddenly
out from behind a cloud,
a long hard rain that washes you clean,
a wildflower at the side of the road,
its color jubilantly declaring,
"I am alive even here, without any care or
comfort, against all logical thought."

Welcome home my dear one.

a time of RELEASING

Heather Doyle Fraser

WEEK 27

This morning.

The grass is adorned with heavy dew,
sparkling in the sun.

Would we shine like that if we were
drenched in our mother's love?

Would we sparkle in the light, our
greatness gleaming in the fresh morning?

Would the dew be enough to wash us clean
and release the burdens of yesterday?

Yes.

When was the last time you ran in the grass barefoot?

When was the last time you rolled all of the windows down in your car and smiled as the breeze whipped your hair around your face?

Maybe it's time to be a child. Maybe it's time to have an experience that reminds you that all of your senses need some nourishment.

Open up the color.

Live in the vibrancy of the 128 pack of
Crayolas.

Put down the Red, Yellow, Blue, Brown,
White, and Black and explore. Search out
Cayenne, Ginger, Periwinkle, Cloud, Clay,
and Slate.

Your range of emotion and feeling and
heart and spirit are begging for more.

a time of RELEASING

Heather Doyle Fraser

What would it feel like to soar untethered to a place where you are gleaming and supple?

A place where you are vulnerable and strong, exuberant and quiet, too...

A place where you are the perfect dichotomy of your soul and everything your heart desires...

Envision this place. Feel it in your bones. Release your judgment around any negativity that comes up. Just allow the unfolding of your imaginings and sit there for a few minutes.

Now, bring these feelings and visions with you into your day.

Sometimes your joy is hiding
underneath the pain and fear.
Dig in.
Open the wound.
It will be okay on the other side.
In fact, it will be better than okay.
Peace, comfort, and contentment are
waiting.

a time of RELEASING

Heather Doyle Fraser

As you reflect on this week, prepare
yourself for an unfolding.

Release
what you do not need
and nurture
what you want to carry with you.

This is your abundant life.

Rest in loving kindness

for I am with you.

Heather Doyle Fraser

WEEK 28

Start today with a practice of gratitude.
What three things are you most thankful
for today and why?

These gratitudes can be simple and
homely, like the steaming mug of coffee or
tea in your hand as you bend your head to
take a sip.

Why? Because maybe it makes you feel
comforted in the still hours of the morning
before you begin your day.

Or your gratitudes can be expansive and
big, like being thankful that you are alive on
this day with whatever it brings.

Why? Because you have the ability to
appreciate that whether the surface of
things appears murky, clear, difficult, or
jubilant, it is all for your greater good.

Write it all down.

a time of RELEASING

When you are in a place of gratitude, your intentions are bigger, more expansive, more hopeful. They evoke a feeling of possibility, potential, and opportunity.

What is your intention for this day? How do you want to see your day unfold?

Setting an intention or intentions for your day is important. If you focus on a feeling, emotion, or a description of what you want to occur it is more likely to happen.

But here is the missing piece — after you set your intentions, you need to identify those actions that will enable you to create the day you envision. And then you write them down too and commit to them.

Write your gratitudes, intentions, and committed actions in a journal or on a piece of paper, and keep it in a special place for you alone.

a time of RELEASING

"WHAT WE CALL
THE BEGINNING IS
OFTEN THE END. AND
TO MAKE AN END IS
TO MAKE A BEGINNING.
THE END IS WHERE WE
START FROM."

—T.S. Eliot

Be kind and compassionate to
yourself today.

If you feel yourself stray from your
intentions and committed actions, gently
bring yourself back
with your breath.

Begin again.

a time of RELEASING

Where is your edge?

Where does your comfort zone stop and
your growth zone begin?

You can feel it now.
Lean into that edge and
look over the precipice of your fear.
Just this small act of acknowledging
your discomfort and fear is the first step
towards transformation.

Look... you've already begun.

I can breathe into the new beginning
before me.

I can lean into the unknown.

I can taste the flavors of uncertainty and
choose to savor them.

WEEK 29

Awake to your greatness!

Using your strengths is one of the keys to fulfillment, joy, and creating a sense of ease in your life.

A CHALLENGE:

Use your strengths in a new way today. Notice how it feels in your body to stretch the muscles that have taken you so far in this life. Observe how you are able to solve problems or create space for yourself in situations that may have seemed difficult before.

Your strengths will not fail you. They can take you even further if you give them the opportunity. Acknowledge your greatness and celebrate their presence in your life.

a time of RELEASING

WEEK 29
DAY 2

What love do you serve?

Where is your purpose, your passion, your joy? Bring it into everything you do and each decision you make, even if it is small right now...

...even if it is just a bloom of an idea or a feeling at this moment.

The flower will follow. You can choose to nurture and care for it.

Step into your new creator mentality. You no longer need the safety of your victim-hood.

Heather Doyle Fraser

Sometimes difficulties and challenges arise in life. No one is immune to them. But what would happen if you greeted the difficult times with appreciation? What if you looked for the gift in every experience to take you to the next place in your life?

What possibilities would open up if you said in the face of adversity,
"Thank you. This is just what I need."

"FINISH EACH DAY AND BE DONE WITH IT. YOU HAVE DONE WHAT YOU COULD.

Some blunders and absurdities no doubt crept in; forget them as soon as you can. Tomorrow is a new day. You shall begin it serenely and with too high a spirit to be encumbered with your old nonsense."

—Ralph Waldo Emerson

a time of RELEASING

Heather Doyle Fraser

Anger or resentment — whether it is directed at yourself or another — is a mask for the fear or pain that sits just beneath the surface. Sometimes it seems less painful to be angry or resentful than it does to feel our own suffering.

Send love and compassion today to yourself and to others. Personify loving kindness in all that you do. You can begin to release and heal these wounds.

Balance on the edge
of willingness and discomfort today.

Peer over edge,
know that you are up for the challenge,
and take the next step.

a time of RELEASING

Heather Doyle Fraser

WEEK 30

Make your practice of loving kindness and gratitude purposeful today. Tell at least three people how much you appreciate them in your life and why.

Be specific and get personal.
Gratitude and kindness are
powerful healers.

Sometimes we go through our days,
moment by moment,
without even realizing it.
We walk blindly through the motions and
the routines of our lives.
And when that happens,
we can miss the magnificence
and the joy of life
that surrounds us every day.

Today, acknowledge the beauty,
the fullness, and the abundance.
Breathe in what you see and hear and feel.
Let yourself truly experience
what is before you in each moment.

Rewire your brain for joy —
see the beauty
and feel it in your body.

Be BOLD.

Creativity abounds
when you give yourself permission
to make mistakes
        and learn from them.

You define your role;
you can make the rules
for how you show up in your life.

Go ahead.
Do something that stretches you.
If mistakes are okay, if you do not have the
pressure of perfection, what journey would
you embark on today?

a time of RELEASING

Heather Doyle Fraser

WEEK 30
DAY 4

What if you acted as if you were already where you need to be at this moment in your life?

Think about what you might accomplish if you just released your expectations of the outcomes — just for today — and enjoyed the process.

There will be a time
when everything suddenly becomes clear,
and your armor is no longer necessary.

I am waiting there,
in that time and place.
I am waiting there
to release you from your small ideas.
I am waiting there
for you to embrace your power.
I am waiting there
for you to embody your joy.

I see you now, closing the distance.
It is time.

a time of RELEASING

Heather Doyle Fraser

"DO ONE THING EVERY DAY THAT SCARES YOU."

— Eleanor Roosevelt

What can you do today to stretch yourself?

Allow yourself to experience the unknown.

Enter into the day
with a sense of wonder.
Look for opportunities. Peer in
when possibility and potential show up —
don't brush them aside.

And then, step into that space
where the potential lives.
Take one step toward your goal...
and then, another.

Your life can be transformed one small
beautiful step at a time.

Heather Doyle Fraser

a time of

EMBRACING

WEEK 31

What is your truth?

Just in this moment.

Share yourself and your truth.
People will show up differently because you
are willing to declare yourself.
They will follow you.

And then,
they will see the truth
within themselves.

Transformation and growth require committed action.

What intention are you willing to commit to and act upon today?

What's your first step?

Today, observe how you view situations in your life — with abundance and hope or with a sense of lack and unease?

Acknowledging abundance and hope feels good.
It brings freedom.
It gives strength.

If the future is not determined today, why not choose to move towards the best possible outcome? Why not choose to move towards abundance and hope?

Even if you do not make it to your envisioned goal, you will have come further than you ever thought possible.

a time of EMBRACING

Is there a pattern in your life that no longer serves you?

What if you replaced it with something that makes your heart sing?
What if you nurtured yourself with loving kindness in a way that you haven't before?

Try something new today, even if it feels awkward at first.

You can change. You can bend.

What if there were more kindness?

What if every day you asked how you could be kinder to yourself and to others?

What would that look like today?

Go through the motions. Imagine every person with whom you will come into contact — throw in some unexpected characters, too! Look into your day and paint a picture of kindness.

Now, imagine yourself in this masterpiece. Imagine the brushstrokes of kindness connecting you to others and to your highest self.

a time of EMBRACING

Heather Doyle Fraser

WEEK 31
DAY 6

Settle in to the stillness.

Know with every fiber of your being that
your purposeful and mindful actions and
words will make a difference.

Gently
turn back to your valued path
with kindness and compassion.

"WITH AN UNDEFENDED HEART, WE CAN FALL IN LOVE WITH LIFE OVER AND OVER EVERY DAY.

We can become children of wonder, grateful to be walking on earth, grateful to belong with each other and to all of creation. We can find our true refuge in every moment, in every breath."

— Tara Brach

a time of EMBRACING

WEEK 32

I feel your hand in mine,
and I am comforted.
And although your hand is small,
your fingers are cool and reassuring.
You have the hope and promise of
youth and a purity of purpose.
You are certain that miracles exist,
that anything can change,
that everything is waiting for you.
And I can believe that, too,
when I remember
you live inside me still.

a time of EMBRACING

What if everything in your life was already a perfect fit?

What if you felt balanced?

What would these changes shift in you?

Today, as you move from one moment to the next, imagine how you would be different.

I am enough just as I am.

I love myself unconditionally as I would love a small child who is unsullied with the worries of the world.

I love myself not for what I have done, but for who I am at the core of my being.

I love myself for all that I am in this moment and all that I am becoming day after day.

I say these words.

I feel them in my bones, in my heart, in the depth of my soul.

a time of EMBRACING

Heather Doyle Fraser

The choice you make today doesn't need to be the last decision you make. It doesn't need to stand the test of time. Today's decision can be for your highest good in this present moment.

Create an intention for yourself. Make a sacred choice and it will lead you to the best right action in the next moment.

This is the place of flourishing.

There is magic here —
in this place,
in this body —
all around me and within me.

I carry this essence
humbly and with joy.

It fills me
until I am brimming
with hope, love, kindness, and curiosity.

It fills me
as I give of myself
and receive love and kindness
from others, too.

It fills me
as I venture out into the unknown.

a time of EMBRACING

Heather Doyle Fraser

"DROP THE IDEA OF BECOMING SOMEONE, BECAUSE YOU ARE ALREADY A MASTERPIECE.

You cannot be improved.
You have only to come to it,
to know it, to realize it."

— Osho

Let the sounds of your life
heal you, soothe you...

~ the quiet whisperings.
~ the raucous laughter.
~ the easy conversation with friends.
~ the quiet tears or heart-wrenching sobs
  met with words of comfort.

A song lives within all of us.
Listen to the masterpiece within. It is a
symphony of knowledge, understanding,
and emotion.

a time of EMBRACING

Heather Doyle Fraser

WEEK 33

WEEK 33
DAY 1

What would you try if failure didn't exist?

Where there is learning,
there is no failure —
it all serves a purpose.

a time of EMBRACING

Today is a new day.

Breathe.
Feel the sun on your face.
Truly taste your food.
Smile with loving kindness
when people pass.

This joy you feel —
even amidst the sorrow
and the surrender —
is Life.

Today, live as if all in your life is exactly what you need to move forward.

No judgment. No blame.

You have the power to nurture what serves you in your life and change what does not serve you.

a time of **EMBRACING**

Heather Doyle Fraser

WEEK 33
DAY 4

What if the sweet and the sad are poured out of the same vessel?

We can say yes to both.

We can surrender and continue to move forward with deep compassion for ourselves and others.

What would you accomplish if you did not internalize the negative stories people tell you?

How would your feelings, goals, and actions shift?

Rewrite your personal stories. Take them back for yourself. No one has the power to write them but you. Don't give this power to someone else. Only you can put a limit on how far you will walk on your path.

a time of EMBRACING

"THE WARRIOR OF THE LIGHT IS A BELIEVER.

Because he believes in miracles, miracles begin to happen.

Because he is sure that his thoughts can change his life, his life begins to change.

Because he is certain that he will find love, love appears."

— Paulo Coelho

What do you believe in?

What do you hold dear?

What do you expect to see unfold around you in your life today?

Sit with these questions in the quiet of your heart and listen.

Let your inner wisdom propel you forward and lead you...

to a place of understanding.
to a place of kindness.
to a place of fulfillment.
to a place of creation.

a time of EMBRACING

Heather Doyle Fraser

WEEK 34

Create the day you envision as your highest self.

Paint a masterpiece of dazzling beauty and step into the colors on the canvas.

What if you chose to experience today without judgment?

No judgment of yourself or others.

What an interesting idea...

No inner critic chattering away providing seemingly endless commentary.

It's a tough task. Allow whatever comes up and then bring yourself back again and again to the stillness of your true being.

Criticism and judgment of others or ourselves is a quick way to suck all the joy out of a day.

What if we replaced criticism with simple observation? What if we replaced judgment with compassion?

That would feel better.

a time of **EMBRACING**

Perfection is an illusion.

We hear this all of the time, and yet, it is hard to release its hold on us and embrace what is right here in the present moment.

Today, begin to release perfection and all the ways it shows up in your life. Take action even if you think you're not ready — even if you fear failure — even if you harbor the thought that you just might not be good enough.

One step. I believe in you.

I am the same
as I have always been
and yet I am different.
I am a timeless well
of wisdom
of learning
of understanding.

I am here living and being,
learning and seeking,
loving in this moment.

Heather Doyle Fraser

"I WILL GREET THIS DAY WITH LOVE IN MY HEART.

And how will I do this? Henceforth will I look on all things with love and be born again. I will love the sun for it warms my bones; yet I will love the rain for it cleanses my spirit. I will love the light for it shows me the way; yet I will love the darkness for it shows me the stars. I will welcome happiness as it enlarges my heart; yet I will endure sadness for it opens my soul."

— Og Mandino

Be mindful and intentional today in all things, and then appreciate what is before you. Happiness, after all, lives in the present moment.

This is just what you need.

Breathe and notice how you feel. Let the fullness of your experience gently embrace you.

a time of EMBRACING

Heather Doyle Fraser

WEEK 35

What if everything is an adventure?

What if the thing you are most dreading today is actually part of your journey and part of the adventure?

Do you want to play today?

Sometimes I play a game. The rules are simple. All I have to do is open my mind and look for the best in people and situations. And then, I let the people I see know that they are making a difference. I let them know that they have touched me in some positive way — whether it's with a smile or a kind gesture or a quietness of character or an effervescence that cannot be ignored. I become a witness to their greatness within.

And while this game is simple, it's not always easy. Even in those difficult moments, though, this game is rewarding. This game turns the things I dread into a life filled with awe and adventure.

We all enjoy a good story. Maybe that's because we are all writers in one way or another. We are all writing the story of our lives, one breath at a time.

Sometimes, though, we forget that we are holding the pen. We are crafting each sentence and paragraph as surely as we are inhaling and exhaling in every moment.

See yourself today for the writer you are. What story would be the best one to tell today? Create that one. Don't settle for anything less. Focus on how you want to feel and then bring that into your life.

That would be a story worth telling.

a time of EMBRACING

Heather Doyle Fraser

Sometimes the inner critic looms before us
cajoling — haranguing — begging us
to stop.

Stop adventuring.
Stop creating.
Stop loving.
Stop living.

That inner critic is just doing its job.
It cringes at uncertainty and desperately wants
you to stay in the safety of sameness. That's
the story it repeats over and over.

Here's the problem, though. That place
of safety and sameness isn't always where
we thrive. It's just a place for us to rest
between dreams.

Sometimes we need a challenge.
Sometimes we need an adventure. Sometimes
we need to stretch and grow. Sometimes to
get to the luscious essence of life we need to
experience the uncertain path.

Slow down

and give your day some love —
wherever you need it most.

Heather Doyle Fraser

WEEK 35
DAY 6

We create our days and our lives —
our realities.

We choose how we respond — to the
people with whom we interact and to the
experiences in which we find ourselves.

Every thought and belief we have is a choice.

Every behavior we repeat and action we take
is a choice.

What reality do you choose to create today?

Be an observer.

Look for potential and opportunity
around you in each moment. Allow the
call of chaos, drama, and stress to go
unanswered — just for today.

Let the song of possibility embrace you and
carry you to your highest self.

WEEK 36

Light would not exist without darkness. So
bless the darkness for its part in your life.

And then,
    bring it lovingly into the light.

In the light, darkness holds no power over
you. You can see its shadow, but it cannot
envelop you. It cannot take away your sight.

Where is your light today?
Look for it and you will find it.

a time of **EMBRACING**

"WHAT LIES BEHIND YOU AND WHAT LIES IN FRONT OF YOU, PALES IN COMPARISON TO WHAT LIES INSIDE OF YOU."

— Ralph Waldo Emerson

We are all catalysts for change.

We inspire others to do things they wouldn't have done without our support and encouragement. We give this to our friends and loved ones, and even our acquaintances without even thinking.

But what if you supported yourself in that way, too? What if you set yourself up for success by showing yourself kindness and compassion? What if you lovingly gave yourself that little push over the proverbial hump in the road?

What would you be inspired to do?

a time of EMBRACING

Inspire yourself.

Let the love inside of you
catapult you
to your highest good today,
encouraging you,
motivating you,
enabling you to do
what you didn't think possible.

How do you feel around the people you interact with on a daily basis? Do you feel uplifted... better for the time you spent with them?

Notice the cues your body gives you as you move through your day. Do you feel ease when you see some people come into the room — does your heart smile and sing? Or do you recoil and feel tension work its way into your shoulders, your back, your hips, or your hands?

Pay attention. And as you do, start to make some conscious decisions about the people with whom you share your time. Begin to increase the time with those that lift you up and decrease the time with those that leave you feeling burdened and less than your magnificent self.

You can support yourself in this way.

a time of EMBRACING

Acknowledge peace and you will feel its comfort around you.

How do you start your day? Do you ease into it with intention or jump in and start swimming in the chaos and action already waiting for you?

A morning ritual is a wonderful way to set the pace of your day...

~ practicing gratitude,
~ meditating,
~ setting intentions,
~ committing to right action,
~ Yoga, Qigong, Tai Chi, Qoya or some other movement that allows you to come back into your body.

Begin with ease.
Find what feels good to you and practice it again and again.

a time of EMBRACING

Heather Doyle Fraser

WEEK 37

What do you do every day?

What has become a habit and pattern
for you? Do you love the patterns in your
life? Do they serve you and set you up for
success?

Take a look.

Really open to what you have created for
yourself. Because you did create it — by
every choice and every moment and every
breath — even if you thought you were
doing nothing. Even that is a choice.

If what you have created isn't what you
want, if it isn't what helps you to be a light
for yourself and others, then perhaps it
is time to embrace another possibility.
Perhaps it is time to embrace yourself and
the life within you.

a time of EMBRACING

WEEK 37
DAY 2

Use everything that comes into your life.

Use it for love.

Use it for learning.

Use it for the gift that it can be.

Allow an opening.

Consistency

can be beautiful and easy.

Heather Doyle Fraser

Why would you wait until tomorrow?

Begin anew in this moment.

Breathe into being.

Today, talk to yourself
with that soft lovely voice
you reserve for your beloved.
Listen as you would to a dear friend.
Witness the beauty within
and then honor it, acknowledge it.

Shore up the foundation of your heart.

And then
begin to build again.
Begin to construct your life
with the beauty you behold within...

And then
notice... how do you feel
when your highest self is speaking?

a time of EMBRACING

Heather Doyle Fraser

"FIND ECSTASY WITHIN YOURSELF.

IT IS NOT OUT THERE. IT IS IN YOUR INNERMOST FLOWERING.

THE ONE YOU ARE LOOKING FOR IS YOU."

— Osho

Your muse is calling.

Let her voice whisper to you in the quiet moments.

Let her song comfort you in the dark moments.

Let her light shine for you when you feel there is no light within you.

Let her soft velvet kisses caress your cheek and touch your heart.

Embrace your brilliance as it comes forth.

a time of EMBRACING

Heather Doyle Fraser

WEEK 38

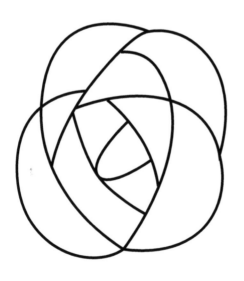

There is a light within all of us.

Sometimes we see its magnificence
and it becomes a beacon for hope,
for love, for passion, and for freedom.
And then other times
we only see a glimpse
and it feels dim, obscured; we feel alone and
discouraged in its waning glow.

I don't know about you, but I would like to
see that light shining brightly more often.
I want to feel the heat from its flame and let
it ignite the passion within me.

Let your inherent greatness and light shine
without apology.

a time of EMBRACING

You can embrace yourself
when the day doesn't seem pretty...
when you don't seem whole...
when the shadow feels like it is too much.

You can embrace yourself
when you are stunningly immaculate
with the pureness of your intent.

You can embrace yourself
when you are lovely in your abundance.

You can embrace yourself
when you give everything to your passion
and when you only give the smallest amount.

You can embrace yourself
when you are lackluster and
when you are brilliant.

You can embrace yourself.

Sometimes... patience.

It could be the most potent and generous kindness you extend to yourself.

Heather Doyle Fraser

Offer...

all of the beauty.
all of the mess.
all of the stillness.
all of the frenzy and chatter.
all of the simplicity.
all of the complications.

I offer it all, and then,

I am ready to receive again.

In the morning
all seems clear
and uncomplicated.
Open your eyes and
look into the rising light.
The day is before you,
full of promise and opportunity.

Anything could change.

I recognize the comfort that comes with
the beginning of a new day. I feel its ease
and allow it to embolden me.

a time of EMBRACING

Heather Doyle Fraser

Bright flowers adorn you, heady and
glorious...

Their soft petals, their saturated color,
their fragrant scent whisper to you
with every breath, leading...

leading you to openness, awareness, ease,
and serenity.

leading you to committed action that feels
right in every fiber of your body.

leading you to your soul's purpose.

What would bring your best today?
What would bring you a sense of luscious
fullness?

Sometimes I need to be soft and yielding,
supple in my movement, my voice quiet in
its knowing.

Sometimes I need to be firm and stand
my ground.

Sometimes my voice needs to fill the space
around me and declare its truth.

And sometimes, still, I just need to be.

a time of EMBRACING

Heather Doyle Fraser

WEEK 39

Your job today:

Create the space you need
to expand into the corners of
your life.

WEEK 39
DAY 2

Sometimes a gray day is best.
The clouds comfort me.
They whisper to me... rest... recharge.

In their shelter, I can sink into the comfort
of an embrace and feel that I am enough.

I can trust the range of emotion within me.

I can inhabit all of the moods of my life
without apology.

I can let whatever is present come forth
and know that this is just what I need.

Today, sit in stillness — for even just five minutes — and listen to your heart.

You can create a life that nourishes and feeds your soul.

What do you want to eat today?
The options are endless.

You could try...
Something spicy or something tame.
Something bursting with flavor —
the juiciness making your tongue tingle —
or something comforting and warm,
embracing your body.

I want to take a bite of everything.
I want to sample it all at some point.
I will choose today and let the food of my
life satisfy me.

Release expectation and
surrender to the process.

Let yourself paint with abandon on the
canvas of your life.
Use your hands.
Feel the paint between your fingers
and laugh.
Remember what it is like to saturate your
moments with vibrant color.

a time of **EMBRACING**

Heather Doyle Fraser

WEEK 39
DAY 6

Abundance is all around us.

Allow your heart to open to the possibility before you.

Embrace the pleasure of receiving.

What would your future self ask of you today?

Heather Doyle Fraser

WEEK 40

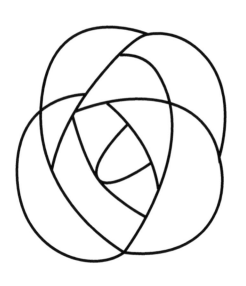

What would bring you pleasure today?

There is remembering in pleasure.

Whatever you learn with pleasure will imprint itself onto your heart and into your existence.

Create a memory of pleasure today.

"MAY YOUR COMING YEAR BE FILLED WITH MAGIC AND DREAMS AND GOOD MADNESS.

I hope you read some fine books and kiss someone who thinks you're wonderful, and don't forget to make some art — write or draw or build or sing or live as only you can. And I hope, somewhere in the next year, you surprise yourself."

— Neil Gaiman

Where are you feeling resistance today?
Where are you feeling ease?

Let's balance between the two
or meet in the middle.
Growth and transformation can feel
exciting and unexpected and challenging
and simple all at once.
Look for the crossroads of your wisdom
and spend some time there.

Today can inspire a growing season.

a time of EMBRACING

Heather Doyle Fraser

What happens when things get messy?

What happens when the vibrant colors of
our lives run together and become muddy?

Mud can be interesting.
Things can grow in the mud.
One of the most beautiful flowers in
existence, the lotus, requires the mud to
take root, to grow, to bloom.

I can embrace the lotus within me.

Quote as mantra:

"AS I EXPAND IN ABUNDANCE, LOVE, AND SUCCESS, I INSPIRE OTHERS TO DO THE SAME."

— Gay Hendricks

a time of EMBRACING

And here it is — the learning again.

This day is just what I need, with all its imperfections and beauty and challenges and ease.

Today, I am a willing participant in the growth and transformation waiting quietly to come forth.
I welcome the duality of our existence here in this physical world.
I acknowledge and embrace all that comes to me for my highest purpose.
I give and receive freely for those I love, for myself... for everyone.

Remember the days
when the blue sky beckoned?
A moment of promise before the snow and
the gray of winter supplanted the sun.
The leaves golden and burnt tumbled down
like coins onto the once lush lawn
now just a cushion for
an abundance of molting.

I could shed my skin like that —
in the crisp breeze
and the sun dappled morning —
against a peculiar blue sky
full of promise.

a time of EMBRACING

Heather Doyle Fraser

40 weeks: A Daily Journey of Inspiration and Abundance

ACKNOWLEDGMENTS

I am so grateful to the many people who have played a part in the writing of this book. My family, dear friends, coaches, clients, and all of those lovely people around the world who allowed me to interview them as inspiration for the creation of this project.

I would especially like to thank:

~ my husband Chris, for being the person I call home, and for always believing in me and supporting me;

~ my lovely daughter Eva, who inspires me every day with her wisdom, her humor, her joy, and her beautiful heart and mind;

~ my parents, who taught me how to say "I love you" without reservation;

~ my sister Stephanie, who has been a teacher for me in many things;

~ my dear friend Bridie O'Shaughnessy, who eased my mind with this project with her attention to detail and copyediting skills; and

~ Danielle Baird, who stood by me, gave my words a beautiful design, and helped me complete this project.

Heather Doyle Fraser

"This is my story. I bring joy and transformation. I shift perspectives and perceptions. I explore possibility, potential, and opportunity. I am willing to dig deep in my own life so that I can help my clients achieve the same transformation and abundance."

—Heather Doyle Fraser

ABOUT THE AUTHOR

HEATHER DOYLE FRASER is a Transformational Life Coach and the founder of Beyond Change, LLC. As a coach, Heather works with highly successful people who are seeking more joy, transformation, and ease in their lives. She holds the space for her clients as they acknowledge their inherent greatness while achieving their goals and vision for an extraordinary life. When she is not coaching, Heather enjoys writing, making art, singing in her celtic band, The Ladies of Longford, and spending time in nature. Heather lives in Ohio with her husband and daughter.

If you would like to learn more about coaching or contact Heather, please visit her website at **www.BeyondChangeCoach.com**.

Coming in January 2016

Deepen your practice with *40 Weeks* by using it in conjunction with the *Companion Journal and Workbook.*

40 Weeks Companion Journal and Workbook will be available for purchase on amazon.com